THE HISTORY OF PHOTOGRAPHY SERIES

Wynn Bullock

GORDON FRASER, LONDON

The History of Photography Series is produced by Aperture, Inc.,
under the artistic direction of Robert Delpire. *Wynn Bullock* is the
fourth book in the series.

Gordon Fraser distributes all Aperture books exclusively in Great
Britain. A catalogue is available upon request.

Library of Congress Catalogue Card No. 76-25727

ISBN: 0-900406-80-1

Manufactured in the United States of America.

"I have always loved light . . . Its manifestations serve as symbols of the greatest secrets of the unknown. Creativity has enabled me to probe and reveal step by step the unknown. Even though I know I can only travel a short distance, every step in that direction is a transcendental experience."

Wynn Bullock devoted most of his adult life to exploring the natural universe and man's relationship to it. The vehicle for his search was the photograph, and he has left a visual and philosophical legacy, a new vocabulary, which will continue to expand as it is subjected to the tests of time. His goal was to see the world, not through societally trained eyes, but freshly and directly. "I didn't want to tell the tree or weed what it was," he said. "I wanted it to tell me something and, through me, express its meaning in nature."

Bullock wanted to break up "pat concepts of reality" and jolt people to new heights of visual and self-awareness by encouraging them to relate to nature directly, unencumbered by traditional modes of visual and mental training. He believed vision included both perceiving and conceiving—and explained, "My interest in defining the sharp difference I feel regarding what we call reality and existence stems from my deep involvement with the mysteries of the existential being of things. I can approach this intuitively and instinctively through the powers of perception far more than through what limited powers of conception I have. I know the powers of conception but I mistrust those powers because of man's insatiable need to clothe life in rules and unrealistic absolutism."

Born in Chicago in 1902, Bullock was aware of his intuitive powers as a child. "I lived a very normal life," he said, "except for one thing. I seemed to have a special sense about people and to see things about them that other people couldn't see . . ."

Bullock's mother, Georgia, was a woman of strong character. She divorced her husband, studied law, and moved to California to pursue a brilliant legal career. As California's first woman superior court judge, she did not hesitate to use her much-publicized position to further the feminist causes to which she was devoted. She allowed her son to exercise his freedom and rebelliousness within wide limits. As a youth, he became disenchanted with the schooling process and preferred to develop his substantial athletic abilities.

While in high school, Bullock discovered he had a good voice and decided to pursue a singing career. He sang for a while with a local hotel band before moving to New York City to further his training and widen his career opportunities. His big chance came in a classical manner. The star of Irving Berlin's *Music Box Revue* fell ill, and his understudy, Wynn Bullock, went on in his place. Coincidentally, President Harding and his wife were present as well as all the reviewers. Bullock was an instant success and, touted as a great tenor, stayed with Berlin's company for three years.

In 1925, Bullock married his first wife, who bore him a daughter, Mimi (1930), and a son, George (1935). A few years after their marriage, they moved to Paris, so that she could attend the Parsons School of Interior Design and he could study with one of the finest voice coaches in Europe. While there, Bullock discovered the work of the Impressionist and Post-Impressionist painters. Sharing their obsession with light, he learned that objects did not have to be represented pictorially; instead, their nature could be revealed by the play of light through reality distortion. Light was alive and plastic; it could create an illusion which came closer to reality than the reality of pictorial works. "The colors didn't actually move, but the paintings made the eye and the mind think they did," he said. Excited that people's minds and perceptions could be stimulated and changed by a static picture, he purchased a small Leica camera and started his initial photographic explorations while continuing to give successful concerts in a number of European cities. His debut at the Salle Gaveau in Paris was reviewed by the Paris *Times*: "It is a voice of beautiful timbre and he uses it with artistic intelligence and discretion. His success seems assured."

Despite his critical success, Bullock grew to feel his voice was limited and decided to give up his singing career. Barbara, a daughter by his second wife, later recalled, "He always wanted to do something creative. He had a beautiful singing voice, but that was, for him, interpretive. He wanted to do something that would connect him directly with the things he was experiencing in himself."

Bullock returned to this country in 1930 and managed his wife's estate in West Virginia during the Depression. Under his management the realty business prospered. After seven years he considered it sufficiently secure to turn over to a bank to administer. He then decided to move to California and enroll in law school. Peter Thompson, former deputy director of the Friends of Photography in Carmel, California, wrote of this period, "His enrollment in law school was an event which pleased his mother, the judge, but which rapidly grew distasteful to him. The logic of the law was not his logic. After several months of conflict with his professors, he simply got up from the class one day, left his books on the desk, and walked down the street to enroll as a photography student at Art Center School, where he completed the four year course in three years."

Bullock soon became dissatisfied with the structured format of photographic education, and only the pleas of his respected teacher, Edward Kaminski, kept him in school. At this time he was deeply influenced by the semanticist Alfred Korzybski, who stressed the principle "the word is not the thing." This principle concerned the idea that words as labels interfere with perception. People are trained to give an object a name; when named, the object represented is forgotten. In other words, language separates people from the reality of events. The familiarity, comfort and safety of words leads to the imprisonment of the mind, something which Bullock was later to try to liberate.

As these philosophical seeds took root, Bullock simultaneously explored the scientific world of photography. He developed the technique of solarizing the negative rather than the print. This process imparted a strange luminosity to the finished print, giving it clarity. Subsequently, he perfected the solarization of the line effect, which reproduced an image with greater clarity and three-dimensionality than ever before. This discovery resulted in the first of several patents.

Bullock was dedicated to his work. His wife felt it was a waste of time. On several occasions, she entered the darkroom and tore up his prints in a fit of anger. This added great strain to an already deeply troubled marriage, and shortly before the death of their cherished son, George, their relationship completely deteriorated; they were divorced in 1941.

In 1942, Bullock joined the army. Continuing his research and professional photography, he at one point photographed German prisoners of war at Camp Cook. He married Edna Jeanette Earle in 1943, following a courtship consisting of visits to boxing matches and Martha Graham dances. Edna was an energetic, diversely talented woman who offered him devotion and stability as well as a humorously critical eye, preventing him from taking himself too seriously. Bullock was released from the army on recommendation of the California Institute of Technology to aid the war effort as a photographic technician for the aircraft industry. After the war, he and Edna traveled throughout California in a twenty-three-foot trailer while he made high-caliber commercial post cards for hotels and resorts. "I didn't have my heart in it," he recalled, "but it was good training and it gave me an opportunity to travel." Their first daughter, Barbara, was born in 1945 and commenced her mini-Kerouac journey bedded down in a dresser drawer in the trailer. The family settled in Monterey in 1946, and Bullock opened and operated a successful photographic concession at nearby Fort Ord. His excellent commercial work received a number of awards.

In 1948, Bullock met and became friends with Edward Weston—a relationship which was deeply to influence his life. Weston's great love for nature and his insistence on experiencing it directly opened a new realm of possibilities. Entranced by the dancing light and vast tonal variations of Weston's photographs, Bullock realized that his formal training, commercial experience and scientific endeavors had boxed him into limited ways of thinking and seeing. He stopped his experimental work, bought an Ansco 8 x 10 view camera and began to explore the countryside with renewed energy.

The countryside, which he defined as "where I came to enlarge myself," included Big Sur and Point Lobos, a wild and inspiring coastline where nature was dominant and never hesitated to reveal her complex glories. The spiritual milieu for the poet Robinson Jeffers, Bullock found its allure both provocative and infectious.

For two years after his meeting with Edward Weston, Bullock's photography was heavily influenced by the former's technique and perspective. At the same time, however, his own vision was evolving, and he began to relate to nature in new ways. The world became for him a constantly changing series of events, forces and interdependent relationships defined by space and time. "I was just photographing what I was seeing on the surface, and then I began to have feelings about the things that I knew existed beneath the surface. I began to examine more about what I was—were things really what I thought they were . . ." As he later explained, "I had this special quality with people and I was able to transfer it to things . . . a kind of unconscious, very deep concentration, a sense that goes on without your being aware of it." Of this time, Barbara has written, "The emphasis became one of learning from things themselves through photography rather than on using photography to develop and prove something already determined."

Bullock believed that visual communication is based on the supposition that a relationship between the inner world of ideas and the outer world of events can be established. He once said, "In the still picture a deeply paradoxical truth exists. Objects can be frozen in time in terms of their specific, physical external qualities, but the mind can respond to these same objects as events in time. This kind of event-seeing involves, of course, the skill of the photographer in expressing symbolically three-dimensional objects and four-dimensional time as well as the awareness of the viewer that permits him to recognize and respond to the symbols that create the illusion."

One of the best ways to illustrate his space/time principle, he believed, was to develop his sense of opposites. The quality of age, for example, was less meaningful without its opposite: youth. Seeking to capture the cyclical nature of the universe—life, death, decay and the regeneration of energy—he juxtaposed youth with decaying forests, and fine, firm skin with aged wood, each quality enhancing the other. These photographs illustrated, through his exquisite sense of visual balance, his belief that opposites are one. Of his photograph "Horsetails and Log," depicting a decaying log surrounded by budding horsetail plants, he said, "It's alive from the standpoint that everything is atomic, regardless of what it is. It's alive in a way that it's going back to the earth, and it's also nourishing the things that are going to grow out of the earth." His daughter Barbara put it this way: "Everything also had a unique time defined by its own functioning and its functioning in relation to other things, past, present, and future."

Family picnics were often vehicles for exploration. His children Mimi, Barbara and Lynne became his models, sometimes subjected to the perils of cold and poison ivy but most often enjoying the experience. Mimi recalled only one occasion when she felt put upon. "Remember when we were in the desert," she said, "and you needed me for scale because of the cacti? You had me standing against the cactus and it got so hot I fainted, and you brought me to and propped me up again."

One photograph of his daughter Barbara, "Child in Forest," was used in Steichen's epochal book *Family of Man*. Feeling it symbolized Lilith, the mythical first woman, Steichen put the picture at the beginning of the exhibition. It evoked intense public reaction, both positive and negative. Some people felt it symbolized new life and the oneness of nature. Others, imposing their limited vision on it, saw the photograph as an image of a dead or molested child. Ironically, another of his photographs, which Steichen labeled "Let There Be Light," was voted the most outstanding in the show by 65,000 visitors to the Corcoran Gallery in Washington, D.C. Bullock was honored but realized its popularity stemmed from many people seeing the diffused sun in the picture as a religious symbol of a cross, thereby exhibiting the very circumscribed mental and visual behavior which he wanted to eliminate.

His nonfamilial, professional models had beautiful, pure white bodies unaffected by sun tans. Succeeding, as few photographers have, in conveying the sensual, soft, tactile and radiant nature of the skin, Bullock's nudes instill in the viewer a desire to touch, as if questioning whether the image is truly flat and two-dimensional. A teacher in Santa Cruz once commented that the difference between Weston's and Bullock's professional models was that Bullock's models looked as if he wanted to make love to them, and Weston's models looked as if he had. Nonetheless, Bullock's nudes were exquisite and created a perfect, unobtrusive level of tension with nature or with old wooden buildings in which the photographs were set.

The photographs made in the 1950's are sometimes referred to as his "nude period." "The period that I was in all during the '50's," Bullock said, "had to do with practically everything at rest." The nudes, almost always enveloped by nature or their environment, were seldom predominant. Wanting to deal with more universal qualities, rarely did he do a portrait or a close-up of an individual; and although he took some fine landscape photographs of the Big Sur coast, he never seriously pursued that direction, either. He believed that in order to do landscapes, one must devote one's life to them as did his friend Ansel Adams. He once said, "People pictures are at a level of abstraction which evokes personal feelings first and truth second. The essence of truth for me is the search for the meaning of the unknown. When I feel a rock is as much of a miracle as a man, then I feel in touch with the universe. Not the object rock, not the form rock, but the light that is the rock."

Around 1960, Bullock exhibited his ability to grow and change when another photographer might have been content to stay securely ensconced in a successful genre. Realizing that he was starting to repeat himself, he gave up black-and-white photography to concentrate on producing color light abstractions. Barbara has pointed out that her father's "cameras changed as his imagery changed." To do his color light abstractions, he used a simple 35 mm Exacta.

To make the pictures, Bullock created a stand to hold several parallel panes of glass. On the various levels, he placed fine, broken optical glass found at the Mt. Palomar Observatory, along with pieces of colored glass, cellophane or anything else that would refract or transmit light. He used all manner of lights and shone them through prisms and the arranged materials from the sides and top and bottom. "I could create thousands of possibilities during the day," he said, "because all I had to do was to move my camera a fraction of an inch or one little piece of glass and the whole character of the picture would change." He found the colored light he operated with to be incredibly exciting in its own right—"not just a tool to illuminate something." He also enjoyed the freedom and control of expression this work allowed. "It is like a painter painting: the color is as close to paint as anything you can get into in photography. You can create a phantasm of forms that can evoke a vast range of emotions."

Bullock produced his abstractions in the form of color slides. Although he occasionally made prints from them, the intensity of the dancing colors was sometimes lost in the transition. One way of compensating for this was to use a high-intensity light attached to a rheostat. He would sit in front of the photograph and adjust the beam of light to the precise level needed to bring out its finest qualities. When the light was right, the most extraordinary nuances of color would emerge sublimely from the print. Although color abstractions had been done before, Bullock took them to new levels of power.

By 1963, he felt he had explored the realm of color abstraction sufficiently and had begun to miss the pleasures and potentials related to working with black-and-white photography. Stopping his color work, he confronted the task of expanding his photographic consciousness in new ways. Pictures evolved which conveyed the passage of time, integrating past, present and future in one image.

One technique he employed was a very long time exposure on scenes with both mobile and static components. By mounting a neutral density filter on an F64 lens, he minimized the amount of entering light while increasing the exposure of the scene to several minutes. The result was often a complex image of soft, luminous movement contrasting with more solid, sharply defined events.

Other techniques involved multiple exposures and superimposed images through which he symbolized time, change and growth. The use of all these processes led to the creation of beautiful, mysterious photographs transcending ordinary reality. Bullock said, "The camera is not only an extension of the eye, but of the brain. It can see sharper, farther, nearer, slower, faster than the eye. It can see by invisible light. It can see in the past, present and future. Instead of using the camera only to reproduce objects, I want to use it to make what is invisible to the eye, visible."

Bullock once asked, "How can you expand unless you search beyond what you are at the moment?" For two decades, he dedicated himself to that search through photography. During the Fifties, he worked to evolve and develop his own vision, and in the Sixties he changed to making color abstractions and exploring light as a force in its own right. He then returned to black-and-white photography and became involved in examining in more depth the space/time qualities of events. By the late Sixties, he was ready to move on again. With renewed energy, he tackled the question "What is real"? and sought to expand his means of perceiving and knowing the world around him.

He now started to produce reversals, a technique of printing the negative image instead of the positive one on photographic paper. Simultaneously, he approached his subject matter more closely, using a Rollei SL66 2-1/4 x 2-1/4 with a built-in bellows and an angle-tilt mechanism for greater clarity. The photography critic Jean Claude Gautrand commented on the effect this way: "It is an extension of this theory of opposites since here new relations are created at the level of the image; shadow becomes substance, absence becomes presence. According to him, the light of these negative images has all the more living energy as it is no longer reflected but absorbed by the object." In addition to these techniques, Bullock printed or mounted his images upside down when he found it could expand his vision.

In his photographs created during this period, events are revealed in new ways: internal rhythms are exposed; light becomes internal rather than external; gravity is defied. If the viewer observes the photographs carefully, he can also train himself in different ways of seeing and thereby expand the manner in which he relates to and is conscious of his environment.

In the last few years of his life, Bullock continued his photographic search. Eager to learn all he could, he was not content with developing new imagery but began exploring the realm of equivalents as a way of expanding and expressing reality. This was possibly the freest period of his career. As he explained, "I just let go and photographed the things I felt deeply, strangely enough about people, but they're non-people pictures . . . I never was able to develop it fully because my health interfered."

His natural intuitive powers plus years of training enabled Bullock to capture the ephemeral. "When these moments came," he said, "I recognized them. It didn't mean that they were continuous moments by any manner or means. But I recognized them, and you better do it, because seldom do the same things happen again." He realized that these moments came most often when he was alone. "I always go alone—with people it would dissipate. I don't want any distractions. I want this one-to-one relationship."

Students often asked him how he made his exposures. "I've been training myself for years to very quickly be able to manage the spatial arrangements of tones and masses." He had absorbed his compositional abilities to such a degree that they came full circle and once again became intuitive. "I usually always shut down to get depth of field. I don't have to worry about lighting, electronic flash, and so forth, because I don't use it." He continued with a chuckle, "And how the exposure was determined—I have a very simple method. It's just, measure it with a Weston meter, and then give it a calculated guess from then on."

In the darkroom, Bullock was a craftsman. He produced prints of exquisite quality sparkling with tonal brilliance. "You can make a beautiful print," he said, "and it can be a record print, but if you print it down just a little bit lower, so that it creates a mood, you lose that record quality, that kind of pedestrian feeling." Many of his photographs have an almost melancholy-dramatic mood to them, but without a threatening element. The mood is evocative, as if something were about to happen, and the viewer is drawn into an anticipatory visual vortex of the photograph.

There is a school of thought that holds an artist says what he has to say with his works and not with words. Bullock was determined to test the Taoist maxim "Those who know do not say, and those who say do not know." He resolved to verbalize the philosophical principles which he experienced intuitively, and this resolution grew as his personal battle with cancer made it impossible for him to continue photography and he came instead to spend many agonizing hours writing and rewriting. "I knew from the start what I wanted to say. I just didn't know how to say it."

Bullock might best be described as a catalytic teacher and philosopher. Even if one did not agree with or understand what he said, one was often forced to think in new ways. Audiences frequently found his lectures difficult to comprehend and he himself was frustrated in making his ideas widely intelligible, but his philosophy has not yet been organized or distilled by an impartial historian and it is the passage of time and closer scrutiny of his work that will determine its significance.

Asked once if he had a legacy to leave, Bullock replied, "The most useful thing to me that I think is most useful to everyone is that they continue to search. Searching is everything."

Wynn Bullock's photographs are ultimately the symbols of the inner workings of his heart and mind as they related to the world around him. His work is the reflection of a gentle man, warm and pure of spirit.

David Fuess

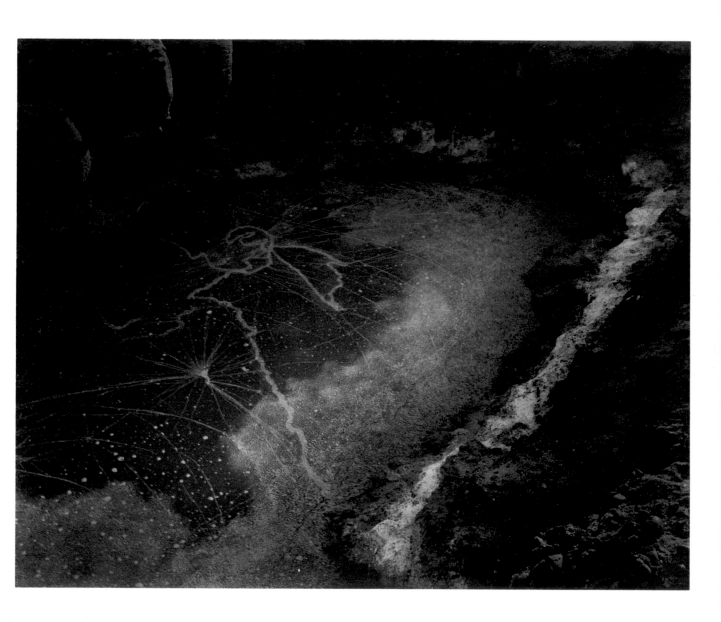

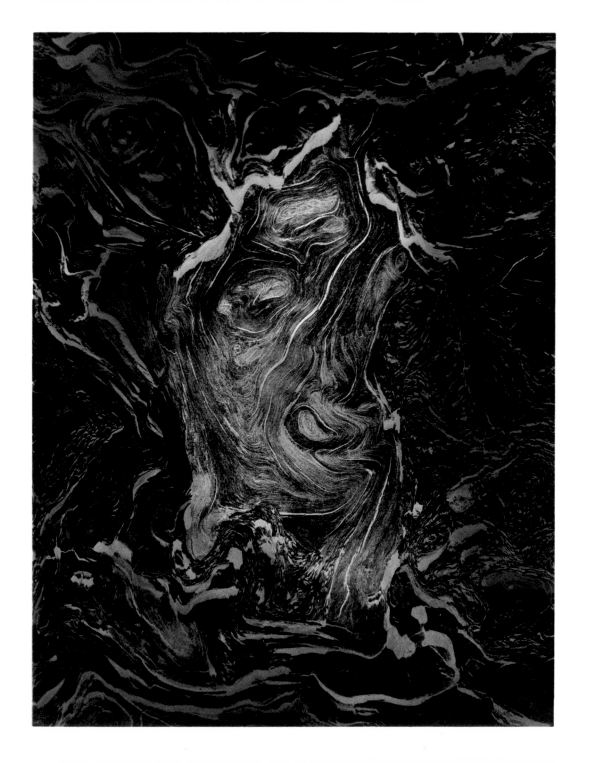

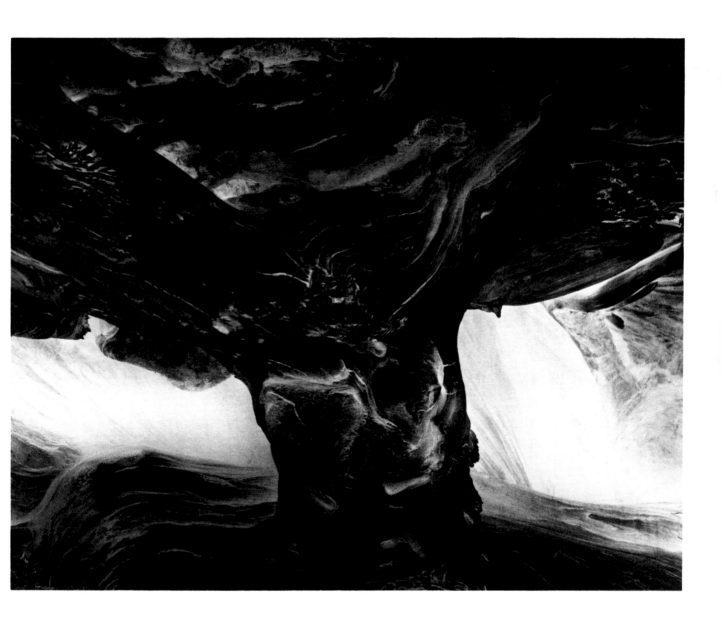

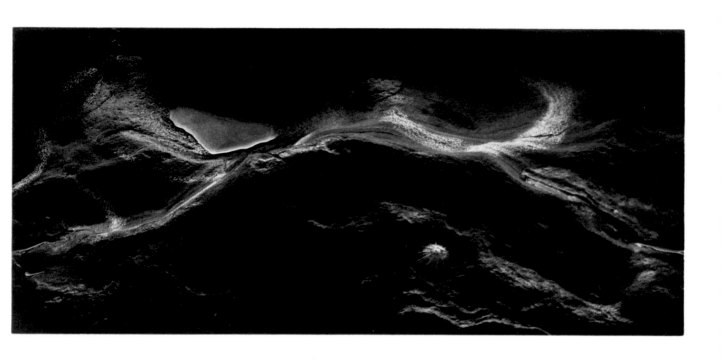

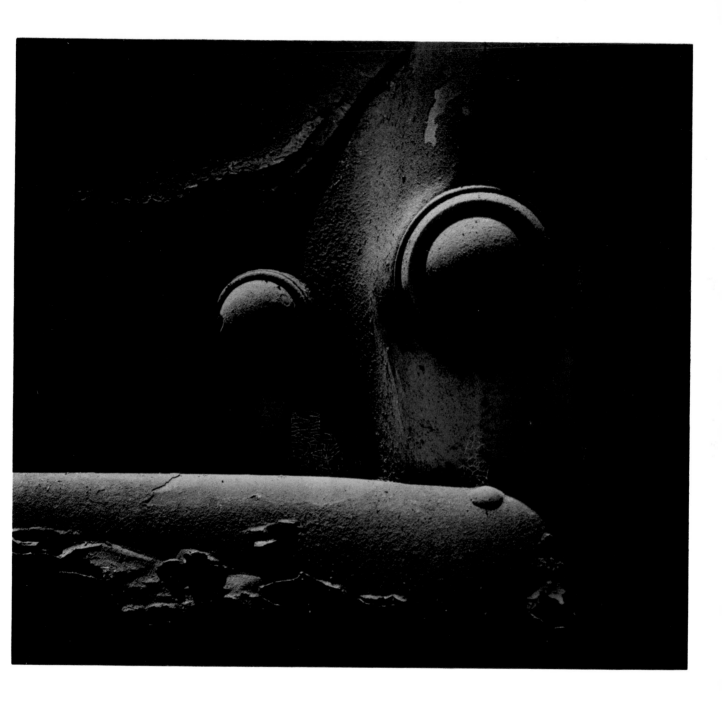

PHOTOGRAPHS

BRIEF CHRONOLOGY

1902. Born Percy Wingfield Bullock, April 18, in Chicago, Illinois.

1907–21. Attended elementary and secondary schools in South Pasadena, California. Developed interest in music.

1921–24. Prepared for career as concert singer in New York. Supported studies by singing, first year as leading tenor, in Irving Berlin's *Music Box Revue.*

1925–27. Married Mary Elizabeth McCarty, of Clarksburg, West Virginia (two children: Mary Wynne, 1930, and George, 1935–42); divorced 1941. Attended Columbia University while continuing full-time singing career and music studies.

1928. Further music studies in Paris. Became interested in visual arts and began to photograph.

1930. Continued voice studies and photography hobby in Milan, Italy, and Berlin, Germany.

1931–37. Managed wife's family real estate business in Clarksburg, West Virginia. Ended singing career; became increasingly involved in photography. Discovered work of general semanticist Alfred Korzybski.

1938–40. Enrolled in Los Angles Art Center School to study photography. Developed close relationship with teacher, Edward Kaminski. Became deeply involved with solarization and other experimental processes. Graduated from Art Center.

1940–41. Briefly studied with Korzybski. Experience deepened beliefs in concepts revolving around principle that symbols are not things symbolized. Beliefs, however, did not yet affect photography.

1941. Work displayed for first time in the first one-man photographic exhibit sponsored by Los Angeles County Museum of Art. Earned living as commercial and portrait photographer in Los Angeles and Santa Monica.

1942. Became managing partner of business primarily involved in handling photographic needs of Camp Cook, a military base near Santa Monica, California. Enlisted in U.S. Army, but retained co-ownership of business.

1943–44. Married Edna Jeanette Earle, of Hollister, California (two children: Barbara Ann, 1945, and Lynne Marie, 1953).

1945–46. Traveled throughout California, producing and selling post card pictures. Settled in Monterey, California. Obtained photographic concession at the Fort Ord military base. There established and, with his wife, managed an organization handling all types of commercial photography.

1946–48. After eight years of research, achieved success in scientifically controlling line effect of solarization and obtained patents for a "Photographic Process for Producing Line Image." Received second U.S. patent on "Methods and Means for Matching Opposing Densities in Photographic Film" in early Fifties.

1948–49. Met Edward Weston; deeply influenced by his photography. Stopped all experimental work and began taking "straight" photographs.

1955. Work included in "Family of Man" exhibition, The Museum of Modern Art, New York City.

1959. Left photographic concession at Fort Ord but pursued free-lance commercial work until 1968.

1960. Began work on color light abstractions.

1963–66. Stopped making color light abstractions although continued for few more years to show color slides. Worked on further refinement of his principles, especially "space/time," as they applied to perception, experience and photography. Gradually resumed black-and-white photography.

1966–68. Began using techniques of long time exposures and superimposed images. Created pictures which evoked for him the flow of depth and change as he was then experiencing it.

1968–70. Retired from all free-lance photography to devote energy to creative work. Became trustee and chairman of exhibition committee at inception of Friends of Photography, Carmel, California.

1970–73. Coordinated old and new into "reality and existence," a principle expressing distinctions and relationships between things as they are in themselves (existence) and man' experience of them (reality). Refined "reality and existence" into principle: "ordering and things ordered coexist yet have independent significance."

1973–75. Took last published photograph, "Wood," in 1973. Enduring effects of cancer, continued philosophical search. To conserve energy while fulfilling many lecture commitments, edited and taped with wife, Edna, two lectures ("The Nude" and "The Concepts and Principles of Wynn Bullock").

During 1975, subject of two films focusing on life and photographic career.

1975. Died November 16 at home with wife and three daughters at side.

SELECTED BIBLIOGRAPHY

Articles about Wynn Bullock

Ornitz, Don, "Natural Nude," *Photography Handbook*, No. 374, date unknown, pp. 42–44, illustrated with Bullock photographs.

Photo Arts, No. 8, date unknown, pp. 56, 92–97, ill.

Booth, C. Weston, "Photographic Horizon," *U.S. Camera*, August 1946, pp. 18, 19, 55, ill.

Tsumuro, Hideo, ed., *Asaki Camera*, No. 12, 1955, pp. 15–21, ill.

Coke, Van Deren, "Creative Photography 1956," *Aperture*, January 1956, p. 12, ill.

Parrella, Lew, "Wynn Bullock," *U.S. Camera Annual*, 1956, pp. 223, 232–37, ill.

Baker, George, "Wynn Bullock and the Camera Eye," *The Argonaut Monthly*, June 1958, pp. 7–10, ill.

Parrella, Lew, "Wynn Bullock," *Creative Camera*, No. 87, 1958, pp. 92–108, ill.

Article about Bullock's one-man exhibit at the Fine Arts Galerie Pierre Vanderborght, *Journal des Beaux Arts*, January 1960.

Lyons, Nathan, "The Sense of Abstraction in Contemporary Photography," *Aperture*, April 1960, p. 111, ill.

Schiegall, Oscar, "But Is It Art," *Reader's Digest*, October 1960.

Bush, George, "Thoughts on Wynn Bullock: The Landscape— An Object of Philosophy," *International Photo Technik*, No. 1, 1961, pp. 40–43, ill.

Williams, Jonathan, "The Eyes of 3 Phantasts: Laughlin, Sommer, Bullock," *Aperture*, October 1961, pp. 96–123, ill.

Herz, Nat, "Wynn Bullock: A Critical Appreciation," *Infinity*, November 1961, cover and pp. 4–10, ill.

Bush, George, "The Nude in Nature," *International Photo Technik*, No. 2, 1963, pp. 113–15.

Pollock, Sir George F., "The Art of Photography," *Amateur Photographer*, August 1966.

Bullock, Barbara, *Wynn Bullock*, a catalogue, San Francisco Museum of Art, 1969, ill.

"Photography Pristine and Pure," *Applied Photography*, No. 40, 1969, pp. 11–18, ill.

Bullock, Barbara, and Uelsmann, Jerry, "Wynn Bullock: Tracing Man's Roots in Nature," *Modern Photography*, May 1970, pp. 84–89, 118, 120, ill.

Jackson, Ruth, "Wynn Bullock: More than Technique," *Camera 35*, 1971, pp. 42–48, ill.

Osman, Colin, ed., "Wynn Bullock: A Retrospective View," *Creative Camera*, June 1971, pp. 190–203.

Badger, Gerry, "Wynn Bullock" *The Photographic Journal*, May 1975, pp. 206–13, ill.

Powell, Lawrence Clark, "To Visit Monterey," *Westways*, January 1976, p. 26, ill.

Hill, Paul, and Cooper, Tom, "Camera Interview: Wynn Bullock, 1st part," *Camera*, February 1976, English ed., pp. 38–40.

Gautrand, Jean Claude, "Wynn Bullock," *Le Nouveau Photo Cinema*, February 1976, ill.

Hill, Paul, and Cooper, Tom, "Camera Interview: Wynn Bullock, 2nd part," *Camera*, March 1976, English ed., pp. 37–42.

Modern Photography, "What's What," March 1976, p. 44.

Popular Photography, "Wynn Bullock, 1902–1975," March 1976, p. 60.

Photography, Year 1976 (Life Library of Photography), "Wynn Bullock, 1902–1975," 1976, pp. 231, 234.

Articles by Wynn Bullock

"Portfolio," *Aperture*, October 1953, pp. 20–29, ill.

"Partial Reversal Line," *The Photographic Journal*, April 1955, pp. 67–69, ill.

"Virtues of Large and Small Cameras Are Evaluated," *Monterey Peninsula Herald's 11th Annual Art Edition*, November 3, 1956, ill.

Article in *Creative Photography 1956*, a catalogue, Lexington Camera Club and Department of Art, University of Kentucky at Lexington, 1956, pp. 10, 11, ill.

"Line Photography," *Medical and Biological Illustration*, April 1957, p. 75, ill.

"Partial Reversal Line Photography," *Medical and Biological Illustration*, October 1957, p. 210, ill.

"A New Concept in Photography," *Carmel Pacific Spectator Journal*, January 1958, pp. 71–78, ill.

"Time's Vital Relationship to Photography," *Contemporary Photography Magazine*, May-June 1960, pp. 6–9, ill.

Article in *The Photograph as Poetry*, a catalogue, Pasadena Art Museum, 1960, pp. 18, 19, ill.

Article in "Three Photographers," *Kalamazoo Art Center Bulletin*, a catalogue, February 1961, pp. 5–8, ill.

"The Fourth Dimension," *Photography Magazine*, September 1962, pp. 42–49, ill.

Article in "Nature Photography," *Pacific Discovery*, May-June 1963, pp. 16, 17, ill.

Photographers on Photography, Nathan Lyons, ed., Prentice-Hall in collaboration with George Eastman House, 1966, pp. 37–40, ill.

Introduction to *The Photographs of Carla Romeike*, 1968.

"Wynn Bullock Nudes," in collaboration with Sir George F. Pollock, Bt., F.R.P.S., *Creative Camera*, June 1969, pp. 206, 207, ill.

Introduction to *Discovery: Inner and Outer Worlds, Portfolio II*, Friends of Photography, 1970.

Introduction to *Edward Weston Portfolio*, Witkin-Berley, Witkin Gallery, 1971.

Introduction to *Wynn Bullock: Twenty Color Photographs*, a catalogue, de Saisset Art Gallery and Museum, 1972, ill.

Books

The Widening Stream, text by Richard Mack, Peregrine Publishers, 1965.

Wynn Bullock, text by Barbara Bullock with selected notes by the photographer, Scrimshaw Press, 1971. (Awarded one of the Fifty Best Books of 1971 awards by the American Institute of Graphic Arts.)

Wynn Bullock: Photography, A Way of Life, text by Barbara Bullock-Wilson, Morgan and Morgan, 1973.

The Photograph as Symbol, by Wynn Bullock, The Artichoke Press, 1976.

FILMS

Two Photographers—Wynn Bullock and Imogen Cunningham, made by Fred Padula, 1966.

Wynn Bullock: Reflections, made by Thom Tyson, 1975. To be released Autumn 1976 by ACC Productions, San Francisco.

ARCHIVES AND MUSEUM COLLECTIONS

Amon Carter Museum of Western Art, Forth Worth, Texas.
Art Association of New England Preparatory Schools, Boston, Massachusetts (headquarters).
Bibliothèque Nationale, Paris, France.
Container Corporation of America, Chicago, Illinois.
Detroit Institute of Arts, Detroit, Michigan.
E. B. Crocker Art Gallery, Sacramento, California.
Exchange National Bank of Chicago, Chicago, Illinois.
Friends of Photography, Carmel, California.
Indiana University, Department of Fine Arts, Bloomington, Indiana.
International Museum of Photography (George Eastman House), Rochester, New York.
John and Mable Ringling Museum of Art, Sarasota, Florida.
Kalamazoo Institute of Art, Kalamazoo, Michigan.
Lincoln-Rochester Bank, Rochester, New York.
Madison Art Center, Madison, Wisconsin.
Metropolitan Museum of Art, New York, New York.
Mills College, Oakland, California.
Monterey Peninsula College, Monterey, California.
Museum of Fine Arts, Boston, Massachusetts.
Museum of Fine Arts, St. Petersburg, Florida.
Museum of Modern Art, New York, New York.
Museum of New Mexico, Santa Fe, New Mexico.
Museum of Photography, Paris, France.
National Gallery, Ottawa, Canada.
National Gallery, Washington, D.C.
Norfolk Museum of Art, Norfolk, Virginia.
Oakland Museum of Art, Oakland, California.
Pasadena Museum, Pasadena, California.
Philadelphia Museum of Art, Philadelphia, Pennsylvania.
Phoenix College, Phoenix, Arizona.
Princeton University, Princeton, New Jersey.
Provident National Bank, Philadelphia, Pennsylvania.
Reva and David Logan Foundation, Chicago, Illinois.
Rhode Island School of Design, Museum of Art, Providence, Rhode Island.
Rhodes National Gallery of Art, Rhodes, South Africa.
Rockford Art Association, Rockford, Illinois.
Royal Photographic Society, London, England.
San Francisco Museum of Art, San Francisco, California.
Smith College, Northampton, Massachusetts.
Smithsonian Institution, Washington, D.C.
Sun Valley Center for Art and Humanities, Sun Valley, Idaho.
Tokyo College of Photography, Tokyo, Japan.
University of Arizona, Center for Creative Photography, Wynn Bullock Archives, Tucson, Arizona.
University of California at Los Angeles, Department of Art, California.
————, Frederick S. Wight Gallery, California.
University of California at Santa Cruz, California.
University of Colorado, Boulder, Colorado.
University of Florida Gallery, Florida Archives of Photography, Gainesville, Florida.
University of Illinois, Urbana, Illinois.
University of Nebraska, Lincoln, Nebraska.
University of Oregon, Eugene, Oregon.
University of Santa Clara, de Saisset Art Gallery and Museum, California.
University of Wyoming, Laramie, Wyoming.
Virginia Museum of Fine Arts, Richmond, Virginia.
William H. Lane Foundation, Leominster, Massachusetts.
Yale University Art Museum, New Haven, Connecticut.

ACKNOWLEDGMENTS

Great appreciation is extended to William and Andrea Turnage who kindly assisted the publisher and the family of Wynn Bullock in planning for this publication and loaning the original photographs from their collection. Barbara Bullock-Wilson—based on her close working relationship with her father—provided editorial advice for the text, the bibliography, and the chronology. The interviews conducted by Thomas Tyson, Peter Thompson, and Amertat Cohn prior to Wynn Bullock's death provided background information for David Fuess whose original article on Wynn Bullock appeared in the *Carmel Pine Cone*, Carmel, California on November 20, 1975.

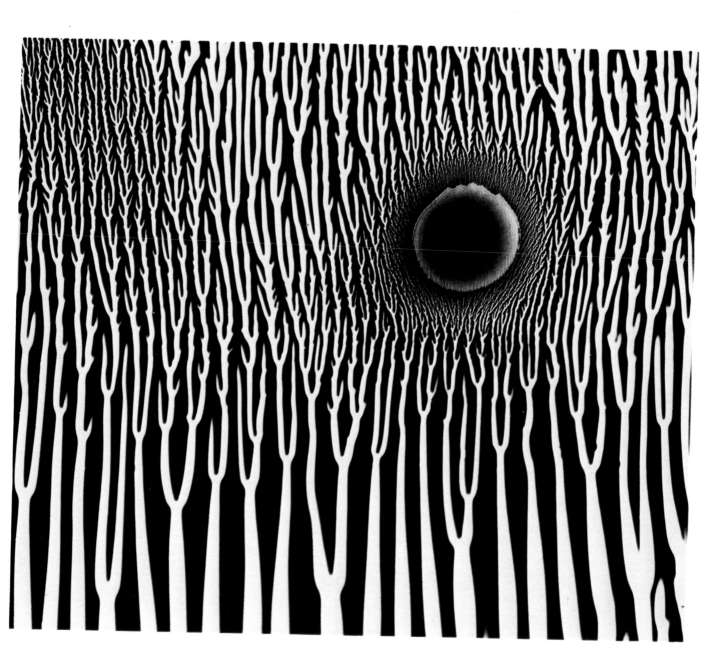